THE TRUTH ABOUT ISLAM

David Eric Williams

Copyright © 2024 David Eric Williams

All rights reserved

The characters and events portrayed in this book are fictitious. Any similarity to real persons, living or dead, is coincidental and not intended by the author.

No part of this book may be reproduced, or stored in a retrieval system, or transmitted in any form or by any means, electronic, mechanical, photocopying, recording, or otherwise, without express written permission of the publisher.

ISBN: 9798880330713

Cover design by: Art Painter
Library of Congress Control Number: 2018675309
Printed in the United States of America

To Honest Americans

CONTENTS

Title Page

Copyright

Dedication

Chapter One: A Politically Incorrect Introduction   1

Chapter Two: The Prophet   7

Chapter Three: The Koran   10

Chapter Four: The Plagiarist   15

Chapter Five: The Example   19

Chapter Six: The Leftism   29

Chapter Seven: The Deception   34

Conclusion, A State Of War   41

About The Author   49

Books By This Author   51

CHAPTER ONE: A POLITICALLY INCORRECT INTRODUCTION

In a July 27, 2014 statement posted at whitehouse.gov commemorating the end of Ramadan, the President of the United States, Barack Hussein Obama, said, In the United States, Eid also reminds us of the many achievements and contributions of Muslim Americans to building the very fabric of our nation and strengthening the core of our democracy.[1] Although this is a politically correct inclusive statement it is also absurd. The truth is, no Muslim has ever made a positive contribution to the "very fabric of our nation" unless it was done in contradiction to their stated beliefs. I realize this is a controversial argument. Many of you may even consider it harsh and unjust. However, as you will see in the paragraphs ahead, Islamic ideology is diametrically opposed to everything we hold dear as Christians and Americans. Truly, Islam is at war with Christianity, traditional American values and the American way of life.

I make no attempt to be politically correct in this missive. I even have the audacity to claim that Western culture is superior to all others. Let me go a step further. I acknowledge and embrace the fact that Western culture is primarily Christian in origin. This is not to say our national identity has sprung from an ecclesiastical institution. Rather, we draw upon the heritage of radical churchmen, parish priests and disenfranchised layman. These rabble-rousers looked to the Bible as their justification for rejecting the status quo. Their demands for equality and freedom found justification from the pages of the Holy Bible not human reason.

As Western culture matured it grew ever more inclusive and tolerant, finding the apex of liberty in the culture and society of the United States of America. The United States is like no other nation on earth. We have never had an established national church (denomination) and we have welcomed people of every nation, creed, religion, color and race to our shores. Unlike many nations throughout history, our heritage allows for disagreement and difference of opinion among our citizens. Indeed, we relish the opportunity to argue our position as preferred over another - whatever it may be. It is ironic that because of our Western, Christian heritage we welcome the followers of Islam to our shores only to find that Islam is entirely inflexible and incompatible with our way of life. To the degree a Muslim is devout he will be unwilling to embrace the most basic traditional American values - values that make the United States of America what it is today - values that have sprung from the Christian religion. This is hard for an American to accept. We are thoroughly indoctrinated with the idea of freedom and really cannot conceive of a worldview that passionately hates freedom. Moreover, we are a people quick to give the benefit of the doubt. We are far too gullible in this regard and so we readily fall prey to the machinations of this alien worldview, seeking to destroy our way of life.

We have fought long and hard in this country to establish these traditional American values. In the pages ahead you will be reminded that many of the things we take for granted today have only been realized in the last generation or so. There were principles included in our nation's founding documents that did not come to fruition for many years. These vales - these rights - are not granted us by a benevolent government but are rights we are entitled to as human beings created in the image of God. Equality before the law, freedom of speech, freedom of religion: these were not handed to us on a silver platter. We must understand that the freedoms we have won over the course of generations could be lost almost overnight. If Islam ever became the predominant worldview in north America the traditional American way of life would cease to exist.

As you read this short work I challenge you to consider how you can help shore up our crumbling culture. The first step you should take is to become informed concerning the Islamic worldview and how sharply it differs from the philosophy of life embodied in traditional American values. Take the time to read the Koran and Hadith[2] and discover for yourself what Islam is really about. Understand as you read these texts, it is not just the rules and regulations that determine the character of Islam. Just as important is the example of Mohammed. Every Muslim on the face of the earth agrees that Mohammed had a superb personality. His life is the perfect example of total obedience to Allah's commands. Mohammed's life is a shining example for us to follow. His life is the complete embodiment of Islam. Mohammed was sent as a prophet to show mankind the best way to worship Allah. During his twenty-three years as Allah's messenger he fulfilled this duty perfectly and meticulously.[3] In other words, if Mohammed thought it, said it or did it, every Muslim must as well. You need to realize we will commit national suicide if we exercise our typical tolerance toward Islam. To do so is to reject our traditional, Christian core values.

It is becoming more common with each passing day to be confronted with intolerance. It is ironic that those two claim the high ground of tolerance and open-mindedness are actually the ones who try and silence dissenting views. The irony is that this leftist attack on animated discussion plays into the hands of the Islamic invaders. Those who demand their view be the only opinion allowed in the marketplace are silencing the voices of those who stand against totalitarianism in all its forms including Islamic tyranny.

In short, I encourage you to become an agent of cultural change. This action is only possible in the context of a Christian understanding of traditional American values. It is in that environment that each of us has the opportunity to make a positive impact on our society. Leftism, in all its forms, hates freedom. Leftism, in all its forms, despises the free exchange of ideas and opinions. Yes, the Left portrays itself as open-minded and tolerant but it doesn't take much common sense to see how backward they have it. It is these same backward thinking people who wish to throw the doors open to Islam. As you will see in the pages ahead this is because Islam is merely Leftism in religious garb.

We need to act now before it is too late. We need to stand up for the traditional American values of equality before the law, freedom of speech and freedom of religion. We need to stop being ashamed of Western, Christian culture and remind ourselves, and the world, that it is the greatest way of life on earth.

DAVID ERIC WILLIAMS

CHAPTER TWO: THE PROPHET

The history of Allah's prophet is shrouded in mystery. Much of what is presented today as historical fact concerning the founder if Islam is the fanciful yearnings of fanatical followers. Muslims consider Mohammed to be the perfect man. He had a superb personality. His life is the perfect example of total obedience to Allah's commands. Mohammed's life is a shining example for us to follow. His life is the complete embodiment of Islam. Mohammed was sent as a prophet to show mankind the best way to worship Allah. During his twenty-three years as Allah's messenger he fulfilled this duty perfectly and meticulously.[4] He is worshipfully described by Islamic adherents as a handsome man of medium build, neither very tall nor short. He had a large head, thick black hair, a wide forehead, heavy eyebrows and large dark eyes with long eyelashes. He had a fine nose, well-placed teeth, a thick beard, a long handsome neck and a wide chest and shoulders. His skin was light colored and he had thick palms and feet. He walked steadily with firm steps. His appearance had the mark of deep thought and contemplation. His eyes gave the feeling of the authority of a commander and a natural leader.[5]

We do know that Mohammed was an illiterate merchant living in Arabia in the late sixth century and early seventh century of the common era. It is reported that he was born into a noble tribe called the Quraish but that didn't mean things were easy for the young Mohammed. His father died before he was born and his mother when he was six years old. After losing his father and mother, it fell to Mohammed's grandfather to look after him, but Mohammed found himself without that protector by age eight as well. Finally, it was his uncle Abu Talib, a leader in the tribe and a merchant, who took custody of the future prophet of Allah.

It was from his uncle that Mohammed found his calling as a merchant. He also worked as a shepherd, but it was his skill as a businessman that attracted the eye of his future wife, Khadija bint Khuwaylid. Khadija was a wealthy widow who was looking for someone to help manage her business affairs. Based upon his reputation for honesty, she hired the twenty something Mohammed on something like a trial basis. It is reported that the young man began to turn a tidy profit for her almost immediately. This so impressed Khadija that she proposed marriage to him. Following the advice of his uncle, Mohammed accepted the proposal and at age twenty five, married the forty year old widow. They went on to have six children and were married for about twenty-five years until the death of Khadija.

Like other Arabic tribesmen of his time, Mohammed originally worshiped a pantheon of 360 gods,[6] of whom Allah was but one.[7] Then, one day, according to the Koran and the other primary religious documents of Islam, the Hadith, Mohammed was visited by the angel Gabriel and given the first of many messages concerning the one true religion.

Mohammed was frightened and confused by this spiritual messenger. He confided in his (then only) wife Khadija and she encouraged her trembling husband to embrace this call to life as an ideological celebrity.

As time went by the spiritual revelations continued and even increased. Also, as time went by, Mohammed began to preach this new-found ideology and slowly gained converts. As we will see, one of the characteristics of Islam that emerged after the migration to Medina is its tendency towards violence.

CHAPTER THREE: THE KORAN

All Muslims believe the Qur'an [Koran] is a unique book. It is the guidance from our Creator for all of mankind. It is the sacred book of Muslims and the main source of law in Islam. Every word of the Qur'an is from Allah. The Qur'an is the final revelation from Allah to mankind.[8] The Koran is the purported perfect record of revelations given to Mohammed in seventh century Arabia. However, it seems this perfect revelation from Allah was subject to the whims of the copyists. As mentioned earlier, Mohammed was illiterate and thus uneducated in the finer points of literary expression. At least one of his scribes helped to remedy the prophet's deficiencies by making suggestions on how Allah's "perfect revelation" should be worded. For instance, when Mohammed had said "Allah is mighty and wise" at the close of a particular verse, his scribe Abdollah bin Abi Sarh, recommended "knowing and wise" as a preferable alternative. Mohammed acquiesced to the scribe. Having observed a succession of changes of this type Abdollah renounced Islam on the ground that the revelations, if from God, could not be changed at the prompting of a scribe such as himself.[9] Abdollah later paid for his temerity. He was murdered on Mohammed's order for apostasy and showing disrespect to the prophet of Islam.

One opinion shared by many Muslims and infidels alike is that the Koran is a confusing volume. Along with chapter titles that often have little or nothing to do with the text, its contents are not presented in a chronological order but are grouped according to length. Although most of the later and longer revelations contained in the Koran appear together, placement in the Koran is no guarantee of its date of origin. In addition, there is little or no historical context in the book. It is simply the record of Allah's reflecting on a variety of subjects. This is problematic because there is no context illustrating the principles of the purported revelation. Thus, the Koran must be taken in an absolutely literal fashion with the supposition that it is literally applied today as it was in the seventh century. As one Islamic apologist has written, the Koran was badly edited and its contents are very obtusely arranged. All students of the Koran wonder why the editors did not use the natural and logical method of ordering by date of revelation. The Koran contains sentences which are incomplete and not fully intelligible without the aid of commentaries; foreign words, unfamiliar Arabic words, and words used with other than the normal meaning; adjectives and verbs inflected without observance of the concords of gender and number; illogically and ungrammatically applied pronouns which sometimes have no referent; and predicates which in rhymed passages are often remote from the subjects.[10]

On the other hand, it is less difficult to trace Islam's trajectory of influence when reading the Koran. Earlier revelations, given while Mohamed's new religion was weak and persecuted tend toward presenting Islam as a meek and mild religion. However, as Mohamed's ideological empire gained in strength and numbers, the revelations recorded in the Koran began to take on a militant and violent character. This is significant because according to most Islamic religious experts, the later revelations given to Mohammed take precedent over the earlier. This is in sharp contrast to the interpretation and study of the Bible. In the Christian Scriptures, it is required that the entire text be considered in any interpretive approach. Thus, no passage from the Holy Bible stands in isolation. Every verse must be understood in the context of the whole thereby placing much of the text in the class of metaphor, simile or illustrative matter.

Meanwhile, such subtleties are unknown to Islam. The general rule is very simple; the Koran must be understood literally, allowing for the most simple (literal) interpretation. Moreover, if Mohammed thought it, said it or did it then that too must be taken literally, providing the normative interpretation and understanding of the Koran for all followers of Islam. The Koran plainly states, whoever obeys the Messenger [Mohammed] is obeying God. And whoever turns away - We did not send you as a watcher over them. ...Whatever the Messenger [Mohammed] gives you, accept it; and whatever he forbids you, abstain from it (4.80, 59.7). This fact is critical in understanding the true character of Islam.

The other primary holy books for Islam are known as the Hadith. The word "Hadith" comes from the Arabic word meaning news or information. It has a special meaning in Islam. It refers to the sayings and doings of prophet, Mohammed and the actions he approved.[11] There are more than one collection of sayings and Mohammedic anecdotes that make up the Hadith. The collection referenced in this missive is Sahih al-Bukhari, one of the Kutub al-Sittah (six major hadith collections) of Sunni Islam. These prophetic traditions, or hadith, were collected by the Persian Muslim scholar Muhammad al-Bukhari, after being transmitted orally for generations. Sunni Muslims view this as one of the three most trusted collections of hadith along with Sahih Muslim and Muwatta Imam Malik. In some circles, it is considered the most authentic book after the Qur'an. The Arabic word sahih translates as authentic or correct.[12] The writings claim to be an accurate record of things Mohammed said or did on a wide variety of subjects. According to Islamic belief, this means the Hadith is virtually on par with the Koran concerning its identity as "Scripture." Indeed, when there is a question concerning the right interpretation of the Koran, it is to the Hadith Islamic scholars turn. In fact, the Hadith is the primary source for the composition and application of sharia. This is why the Hadith is such interesting reading to Westerners. Within its pages are found prohibitions against silk garments for men (1.8.372, 2.23.331, 4.54. 471), visual art (7.72.834) musical instruments (7.69. 494) and death for apostates (4.52.260, 9.83.17, 9.89. 271 etc). Moreover, if a baby urinates on your garments, you are to follow the example of Mohammed and wash the spot with water - and keep wearing the garment without further washing (Hadith, 1.4.223). When a man relieves himself, he must never touch his private parts with his right hand nor clean himself after defecation with his right hand (7.69.534). If he uses stones to clean himself after elimination, it must be an odd number of stones (1.4.162). Great stuff!

CHAPTER FOUR: THE PLAGIARIST

Charges of plagiarism and fabrication were leveled at Mohammed from the very beginning of his career as the prophet of Allah. Mohammed's opponents claimed his fresh revelations where nothing but myths of the ancients (Koran, sura 6.25, 8.31, 23.83, 25.5) and that he recited a jumble of dreams and that he made it up (21.5). It is interesting to note that there was not a "canonical" form of the Koran until well after the death of Allah's prophet. Even the most devout Muslim usually admits that if any original ever existed, it was lost and the text available today is based on the recollections of Mohammed's earliest followers.

If you have an acquaintance with Christian and Jewish Scripture, you will find some things seem familiar as you read the Koran. No, it won't be teachings about the universal brotherhood of man or a command to love your enemies and do good to those who hate you. Instead you encounter stories lifted from orthodox and heterodox Christian writings or Jewish literature supplied with a Muslim twist. As one Muslim writer said, all the moral precepts of the Koran are self-evident and generally acknowledged. The stories in it are taken in identical or slightly modified form from the lore of the Jews and Christians, whose rabbis and monks Mohamed had met and consulted on his journeys to Syria, and from the memoirs conserved by descendants of the peoples of Ad and Thamud.[13]

You'll have to pay close attention however. The familiar stories of Jewish Scripture - Adam and Eve, Cain and Able, Noah and his ark, Joseph in Egypt and so on, seem to miss the point somehow. For instance, the story of Cain and Able as it appears in the Koran draws upon the Jewish rabbinic tradition saying Cain's murder of his brother was like the murder of an entire race. In Jewish tradition, this is so because God's word to Cain references Able's "bloods" as in, "your brother's bloods cry out to Me (God) from the ground." "Bloods" is understood to mean Abel's potential descendants. The Koran doesn't quite get it. In Mohammed's retelling, the claim is made that killing Abel was like killing an entire race - with no reference to "bloods" or any other explanation as to why the death of one man represented the death of a multitude. Hence, the Koran's account reads like a retelling of the story by a man who has listened to it attentively, but has nonetheless left out one salient detail.[14]

One interesting detail is that the reference to

"bloods" is not actually found in the Hebrew scripture. It is only found in the oral tradition of the Jewish Rabbis (later written down in the Talmud). Mohammed's clumsy piracy is what one would expect of someone unable to read or write and yet familiar with the oral teaching of seventh century mainstream Jewish doctrine. Clearly Mohammed had heard the then current teaching of the Jewish rabbis and incorporated it into his own holy book. The same is true in the retelling of the orthodox and heterodox Christian stories.

In the second century non-canonical Gospel of Thomas, there is a story of the boy Jesus fashioning sparrows out of clay and then, with a clap of his hands, bringing them to life so they fly away. The Koran draws from this myth but fumbles in the reckoning. In the revelations of Mohammed, the angel Gabriel tells Mary that one day her son Jesus will chastise those who reject Islam by saying, I have come to you with a sign from your Lord. I make for you out of clay the figure of a bird, then I breathe into it, and it becomes a bird by God's leave. And I heal the blind and the leprous, and I revive the dead, by God's leave. And I inform you concerning what you eat, and what you store in your homes. In that is a sign for you, if you are believers (3.49 see also 5.110). Indeed, in this passage alone, Mohammed draws from the heterodox Gospel of Thomas, along with the canonical texts of Matthew Mark, Luke and John. Clearly he had heard these things from the

Christian teachers he rubbed shoulders with while living in Mecca.

Even more strange is the common Islamic claim that Alexander the Great was a proto-Islamist.[15] According to Islamic teaching, Alexander was Muslim before Muslim was cool.

CHAPTER FIVE: THE EXAMPLE

When we move beyond reading the Koran and Hadith as light entertainment, we are soon confronted by the hard cold fact that Islam is a violent, intolerant, deceptive religion.

Unlike Christianity, there is no well-developed doctrine of salvation in the religion of Islam. According to the Koran and the Hadith, salvation is earned by gaining Allah's favor through acts of obedience, primarily through jihad. However, what this entails is not entirely clear apart from the all-consuming need for Muslims to defend the Islamic faith of Allah and Mohammed at all costs. This is the one consistent theme that runs through the Koran and Hadith.

Mohammed's attitude toward infidels is anything but charitable. As mentioned, it is true that early in the history of Islam, Mohammed taught his followers to avoid provoking the ire of those who opposed his new ideology. This kind and gentle approach is reflected in the early Koranic writings. However, once Mohammed gained power and influence, the pacific approach gave way to a much more militant expression of the Islamic faith. Remember, the way one defends Islam is to imitate Mohammed, the apostle of Allah, the prophet of Islam. Whatever Mohammed did equals normative behavior for the followers of Islam.

Thus, there really is no such thing as moderate Islam. The real divisions between devout Muslims and non practicing Muslims because a true follower of Allah must emulate the example of Mohammed in every way in order to please his god. And as we shall see in the paragraphs ahead Mohammed eventually arrived at the point where he extended no quarter to those who deny or disagree with Islam.

Time and again we are told the Islamic terrorism taking place around the world on a daily basis is an aberration. However, if we understand the subtleties of Islam concerning infidels, Islamic terrorism makes a perverse sort of sense. You see, a good Muslim is one who contends for the faith, always defending Islam with his own person and his worldly goods. When Islam is resisted - even by words or nonviolent action - it is considered an attack on Allah and his prophet. Therefore, violent action against those who do this is justified. Moreover, according to the Muslim holy books, any nation that does not submit to Islamic law is likewise at war with Islam. The goal of Islam is to subdue or destroy all infidels.

At Medina, Mohamed and his fellow refugees found it difficult to earn a living and soon resorted to plundering caravans for livelihood, a practice which they justified upon the ground that the merchants were idolaters and unbelievers. Mohamed strengthened his authority and provided funds for his followers by exiling hostile Jewish clans and confiscating their property. Other obnoxious individuals were assassinated, and once some six hundred Jews who would not accept Islam were executed in cold blood and their women and children were sold into slavery. Thus the new religion began early to take on the ruthless and sordid features of conquest and tribute, and the persecuted prophet rapidly transformed himself into religious despot and national legislator.[16]

Hence, all polytheistic idolaters (such as Hindus) must be resisted at all times in every place; the same is mandated for Christians and Jews. According to the Islamic holy books, the only good Christian or Jew is the Christian or Jew who realizes their faith is nothing more than a form of proto-Islam. Once they realize the truth they will convert to Islam, thereby becoming Muslims. So, the worst of sins are infidelity (kufur) and polytheism (shirk) which constitute rebellion against Allah, the creator. To eradicate these, Muslims are required to wage war until there exists none of it in the world, and the only religion is that of Allah.[17]

There is no imaginative theorizing in this theology. It is simply a rephrasing of the words of the Islamic holy books. The following is a sampling of what every good Muslim must do.

And fight in the cause of God those who fight you, but do not commit aggression; God does not love the aggressors. And kill them wherever you overtake them, and expel them from where they had expelled you. Oppression is more serious than murder. But do not fight them at the Sacred Mosque, unless they fight you there. If they fight you, then kill them. Such is the retribution of the disbelievers. And fight them until there is no oppression, and worship becomes devoted to God alone. But if they cease, then let there be no hostility except against the oppressors (Koran, sura 2.190-193).

Fighting is ordained for you, even though you dislike it. But it may be that you dislike something while it is good for you, and it may be that you like something while it is bad for you. Allah knows, and you do not know (2.216).

Fight in the cause of Allah, and know that Allah is Hearing and Knowing (2.244).

The punishment for those who fight Allah and His messenger, and strive to spread corruption on earth, is that they be killed, or crucified, or have their hands and feet cut off on opposite sides, or be banished from the land. That is to disgrace them in this life; and in the Hereafter they will have a terrible punishment (5.33).

Fight them until there is no more persecution, and religion becomes exclusively for Allah. But if they desist - Allah is Seeing of what they do (8.39).

When the Sacred Months have passed, kill the polytheists wherever you find them. And capture them, and besiege them, and lie in wait for them at every ambush. But if they repent, and perform the prayers, and pay the alms, then let them go their way. Allah is Most Forgiving, Most Merciful. Fight those who do not believe in Allah, nor in the Last Day, nor forbid what Allah and His Messenger have forbidden, nor abide by the religion of truth - from among those who received the Scripture - until they pay the due tax, willingly or unwillingly ...And fight the polytheists collectively, as they fight you collectively, and know that Allah is with the righteous (9.5, 29, 36).

Allah loves those who fight in His cause (61.4).

You will note that according to the Koran, oppression is worse than murder (2.190). In other words, it is worse for non-Muslims to oppress a Muslim than it is for a Muslim to kill his oppressor. And according to the Islamic holy books, to disagree with Islam and speak against it is to oppress or persecute it. Moreover, those who oppress or persecute Islam must be fought until they are all gone.

And now, from the Hadith.

Allah's Apostle said: "I have been ordered (by Allah) to fight against the people until they testify that none has the right to be worshiped but Allah and that Muhammad is Allah's Apostle, and offer the prayers perfectly and give the obligatory charity, so if they perform a that, then they save their lives and property from me except for Islamic laws and then their reckoning (accounts) will be done by Allah" (1.2.24).

Allah's Apostle was asked, "What is the best deed?" He replied, "To believe in Allah and His Apostle (Muhammad). The questioner then asked, "What is the next (in goodness)? He replied, "To participate in Jihad (religious fighting) in Allah's Cause" (1.2.25).

A man came to the prophet and asked, "O Allah's Apostle! What kind of fighting is in Allah's cause? (I ask this), for some of us fight because of being enraged and angry and some for the sake of his pride and haughtiness." The prophet raised his head (as the questioner was standing) and said, "He who fights so that Allah's Word (Islam) should be superior, then he fights in Allah's cause" (1.3.125).

Allah's Apostle said, "I have been ordered to fight the people till they say: 'None has the right to be worshiped but Allah.' And if they say so, pray like our prayers, face our Qibla and slaughter as we slaughter, then their blood and property will be sacred to us and we will not interfere with them except legally and their reckoning will be with Allah." Narrated Maimun ibn Siyah that he asked Anas bin Malik, "O Abu Hamza! What makes the life and property of a person sacred?" He replied, "Whoever says, 'None has the right to be worshiped but Allah', faces our Qibla during the prayers, prays like us and eats our slaughtered animal, then he is a Muslim, and has got the same rights and obligations as other Muslims have" (1.8.387).

I asked the prophet, "What is the best deed?" He replied, "To believe in Allah and to fight for His Cause" (3.46.694).

The prophet said, "...Paradise has one-hundred grades which Allah has reserved for the Mujahidin who fight in His Cause, and the distance between each of two grades is like the distance between the Heaven and the Earth." (4.52.48).

Allah's Apostle said, "Allah welcomes two men with a smile; one of whom kills the other and both of them enter Paradise. One fights in Allah's Cause and gets killed. Later on Allah forgives the 'killer who also get martyred (In Allah's Cause)" (4.52.80).

History tells us that Mohammed and his followers took Allah's commands to fight in his cause very literally. Muhammad himself arranged sixty five military campaigns in the last ten years of his life, leading twenty seven of them himself. As the prophet of Allah gained in power and influence it became clear that he encouraged war not to defend Islam but to impose it upon others.

After Muhammad's death, war immediately broke out between the Muslims and former allied tribes that wanted to part ways with Islam. There was a universalism implicit in Mohamed's teaching and actions: he claimed universal authority, the haram which he established had no natural limits; in his last years military expeditions had been sent against the Byzantine frontier lands, and he is supposed to have sent emissaries to the rulers of the great states, calling on them to acknowledge his message. When he died, the alliances he had made with tribal chiefs threatened to dissolve; some of them now rejected his prophetic claims, or at least the political control of Medina. Facing this challenge the community under Abu Bakar affirmed its authority by military action.[18]

Abu Bakr, the prophet's successor, declared the wayward tribes apostate and proceeded to kill all who fell into his hands. It was only through violence and threats of violence that the Islamic empire survived the tumultuous years after Mohammed's death. But it wasn't only war against apostates that shook the kingdom of Allah, there was intrigue and civil war and among the faithful as well. In the twenty five years following Mohammed's death, four caliphs in turn took charge of the Muslim empire; three out of four were murdered by rival factions within Islam. These civil wars, assassinations and intrigue are the origin of the many coteries within Islam today - each with it's own accepted line of succession from the prophet of Allah to the present day and each with its own ideological peculiarities. The Koran and Hadith are very clear concerning Mohammed's belief that followers of Allah should do battle against unbeleivers. With this clear message from Allah and his apostle, Muslims embarked on a fourteen hundred year orgy of warfare, plundering and enslavement. Many contemporaries of Muhammad lived to see Islam wage war on every major religion in the world. Hindus, Christians, Jews, Zoroastrians, and Buddhists were all targets of the jihad.

Muslim jihad conquered much of the Christian world before Europeans began to fight back. The Crusades were a response to Muslim aggression ranging from from Syria all the way to Spain, and across North Africa. Islamic warriors enslaved countless Christians along with millions of pagan Africans as spoils of war. Arab slavers continued to ply their trade for 1300 years. It did not come to an end until Christian nations forced the Islamic world to cease and desist. Yet, the practice was not really ended but driven underground. Indeed, ISIS has openly revived the Islamic custom of making slaves of conquered people and has even issued a fatwa concerning the proper treatment of slave girls in this modern era.[19]

Contrary to leftist critics of all religions except

Islam, the "peaceful religion" of Allah is the only organization calling itself a religion that consistently sponsors terror. And it is not the less devout Muslim we should worry about but those who are deeply devoted to Islam and accept the words of the Koran at face value. These are the ones who are purists and follow most closely the mandate to imitate Mohammed in everything and in every way.

As we have seen, the holy books of Islam are filled with admonitions to do violence against those who reject Allah and his Prophet - and we have just scratched the surface.

CHAPTER SIX: THE LEFTISM

Many Americans are baffled by the warm fuzzy feelings much of the political class has for Islam. To most American citizens, there seems to be little or no ideological common ground between the beliefs of the left leaning ruling elite and Islamic doctrine. Yet, upon closer examination it is apparent that Islam is just leftist ideology in religious garb.

Erik Von Kuehnelt-Leddihin spent his lifetime researching leftism. In his magnum opus, Leftism Revisited,[20] he provided a lengthy list of characteristics common to all leftist movements or organizations. If we use a portion of his list as a guide, the leftist character of Islam quickly becomes apparent.

Islam and Leftism justify the struggle against extraordinary people, against "privileges."

Islam and Leftism promote one form of freedom: freedom below the belt, with Islam allowing this "freedom" for men only.

Islam and Leftism view conformism as a vital principle.

Islam and Leftism promote dynamic monolithism: state, society, people become one.

Islam and Leftism promote the glorification of revolution, revolt and upheaval.

Islam and Leftism both practice persecution, subjection, or control of all religious bodies other than their own.

Islam and Leftism are antiliberal with a hatred of freedom.

Islam and Leftism embrace a rigid ideology enforced by the state - a complete anti-image of "The Enemy."

Islam and Leftism both promote an ideological one-party state.

Islam and Leftism are characterized by brute force and terror, not authority of law, but as power intrinsic to the ideology.

Islam and Leftism are totalitarian: all spheres of life forcibly pervaded by one doctrine.

Islam and Leftism are messianic: not a personal messiah but a group, class or ideology brings salvation.

Islam and Leftism are materialistic and sensualistic: consider Islam's concept of heaven for instance and its preoccupation with bodily functions.

Always keep in mind that there is no compromise in leftist ideology. Moreover, it is impossible to defeat leftism on the intellectual battlefield because it is a world view immune to logical argument. Instead it is a spiritual battle; it is the Gospel of Jesus Christ alone that changes a man's heart.

It has been said that Leftism is a form of mental illness and I think it probably is - as anyone who has tried to point out the inherent inconsistencies of leftism to a socialist friend knows. This same stubborn hubris is characteristic of Islam as well. If you need to be convinced of this fact, try this little exercise; ask a Muslim acquaintance if he agrees with the Islamic teaching demanding death to infidels. He will likely reply that there is no such requirement in the Islamic holy books. At that point, whip out your personal copy of the Koran and turn to sura 9.5 and read, kill the polytheists wherever you find them. And capture them, and besiege them, and lie in wait for them at every ambush. He will likely say that is a mistranslation of the Arabic text. You will then point out you are reading from an approved translation. His response will probably be that you are misinterpreting the text. At which point you will want to reference anyone of the many noted Islamic scholars who interpret the text quite literally as you have. His final response as he shakes his head and walks away will probably be to call you a racist, bigoted Westerner who lacks the intelligence and sophistication to appreciate one of the world's great religions.

This unrestrained hubris is exhibited in the convoluted logic Muslims commonly use to defend Islamic aggression. According to Muslim apologists, Islam is the only true freedom and the teachings of Mohammed require Muslims to rid the world of oppression so people are free to decide for themselves if they wish to become Muslims or not. Thus, there are many practical obstacles in establishing Allah's rule on Earth, such as the power of the state, the social system and traditions and, in general, the whole human environment. Islam uses force only to remove these obstacles so that there may not remain any wall between Islam and individual human beings, and so that it may address their hearts and minds after releasing them from these material obstacles, and then leave them free to choose to accept or reject it.[21] In other words, Islam must destroy rival civilizations in order to free the people living in those societies from non-Islamic influence.

Moreover, it is the conviction of devout Muslims that even those nations that "leave well enough alone" are not exempt from the jihadist onslaught: It may happen that the enemies of Islam may consider it expedient not to take any action against Islam, if Islam leaves them alone in their geographical boundaries to continue the lordship of some men over others and not extend its message and its declaration of universal freedom within their domain. But Islam cannot agree to this unless they submit to its authority by paying jizyah [subordination tax] which will be a guarantee that they have opened their doors for the preaching of Islam and will not put any obstacle in its way through the power of the state.[22]

This is how Muslims understand the religion of peace. Peace is defined as Islam in ascendancy. Freedom is defined as the elimination of any and all rivals to Islam. Only a mind in the grip of ideological lunacy can accept this irrational definition of peace and freedom.

CHAPTER SEVEN: THE DECEPTION

It has been said that Islam is a religion that gains converts at the point of a sword. This is not exactly true. In the perfect Islamic world, Muslim armies gain territory for the Islamic State and everyone who comes under their control is given a choice. They are told they must convert to Islam or, if they choose to reject the faith, they will live as second-class citizens. This applies specifically to Jews and Christians. They are allowed to remain in their faith but only if they pay certain taxes and, according to the Islamic holy books, are made to feel humiliated and subdued (Koran, sura 9.29). The conditions forced upon the dhimmis (non-Muslim people constrained to submit to the rule of Islamic law) were codified in what is known as the pact of Umar. In general they were not forced to convert, but they suffered from restrictions. They paid a special tax; they were not supposed to wear certain colors; they could not marry Muslim women; their testimony was not accepted against that of Muslims in the law courts; their houses or places of worship should not be ostentatious; they were excluded from positions of power[23] could not restore a place of worship that needed restoration, could not use such places for the purpose of enmity against Muslims, could not proselytize, could not prevent members of their own community from converting to Islam, were required to provide room and board for Muslims for at least three days when asked, move from a place where they were sitting if a Muslim chose to sit there, could not dress in a way similar to a Muslim and so on.[24] These restrictions and more are the norm wherever Islamic law is enforced.

One of the reasons "moderate Muslims" deny the true character of Islam is because Muslims are instructed to deceive the enemies of Islam when they are not in a position to gain the upper hand. This is known as the doctrine of taqiyya. And for Islam, the upper hand is always predicated upon the ascendancy of Islam.

Two of the primary texts allowing deception among the followers of Allah are found in the Koran: Believers are not to take disbelievers for friends instead of believers. Whoever does that has nothing to do with God, unless it is to protect your own selves against them. God warns you to beware of Him. To God is the destiny (sura 3.28) and whoever renounces faith in God after having believed - except for someone who is compelled, while his heart rests securely in faith - but whoever willingly opens up his heart to disbelief - upon them falls wrath from God, and for them is a tremendous torment (16.106). Regarding 3:28, the Islamic scholar Ibn Kathir (1301-1373) wrote: "Whoever at any time or place fears their (infidels') evil, may protect himself through outward show." As proof of this, he quotes Muhammad's companions. "Abu Darda said: 'Let us smile to the face of some people while our hearts curse them.' Al-Hassan said: 'Doing taqiyya is acceptable till the day of judgment.'"

In other words, don't befriend infidels unless it is done in deceit to protect yourself (and further the cause of Islam). In addition, renouncing your faith is okay if it is a deception to protect yourself (and further the cause of Islam).

The Hadith agrees that there are times when lying is permissible: she heard Allah's Apostle saying, "He who makes peace between the people by inventing good information or saying good things, is not a liar" (3.49.857) and Narrated by 'Ali: Whenever I tell you a narration from Allah's Apostle, by Allah, I would rather fall down from the sky than ascribe a false statement to him, but if I tell you something between me and you (not a Hadith) then it was indeed a trick (i.e., I may say things just to cheat my enemy) (9.84.64).

Granted, many of us tell "white lies" in order to keep peace between family and friends. But in the Christian religion, at least, there are no Bible references where permission is granted to do so. Moreover, most of us understand that deception of enemies in time of war is common practice among all nations. But as we will see, taqiyya embodies more than that.

The origins of taqiyya are found in the Shia - Sunni split in Islam. The Shia branch of the religion insists that religious authority resides in the family of Ali, a cousin and son in law of the prophet (Shia is an abbreviation of Shiatu ?Ali, meaning "followers of Ali"). Meanwhile the Sunnis claim to be true followers of Mohammed (Sunni comes from the word "sunna" or "example," as in followers of the example of Mohammed). After the Islamic civil wars of 656 to 661 AD, the Sunnis became a majority within Islam and a general persecution of Shias ensued that continues to this day. The doctrine of taqiyya became crucial to the survival of the Shia minority. Thus, based upon the texts cited above, the Shia minority (about 10% of all Muslims) believes they are morally justified in deceiving the Sunni majority as a means of survival.

Religious freedom as we understand it does not exist in Muslim states and a restriction on unapproved religious practice extends to the minority Shia. For instance, in Saudi Arabia, Shias are considered heretics and infidels and are often persecuted - if discovered. Indeed, many Muslim clerics in Saudi Arabia have issued fatwas authorizing the murder of

Shias Under these circumstances, Shias commonly practice taqiyya. They outwardly give abeyance to Sunni beliefs while inwardly they remain Shia. Thus, after 1,400 years of practicing taqiyya, Shias are often accused of being habitual liars by Sunnis.

On the other hand, Sunnis have had little reason to lie about their faith over much of the past 1400 years. With the migration of thousands of Sunni Muslims to the Western world those circumstances have changed. What was once considered a Shia fault is increasingly understood as a broader Muslim duty; deception for the sake of Islamic ascendency.

Once the need to practice taqiyya arose for Sunnis, there was ample precedent for doing so in the life and example of Mohammed. As we have seen, the Koran and Hadith clearly teach that deceit is permissible in certain situations. Moreover, it is not the record of Mohammed's words alone that supply doctrinal support for taqiyya; his actions do so as well.

In 627 AD, the early Muslims found themselves in a conflict with a confederation of non-Islamic tribes and were under siege near present day Medina. One of the "confederates," Naim bin Masud, found his way to the Muslim camp and subsequently became a Muslim believer. He was then counseled by Mohammed to return to the camp of his former comrades and hide his new beliefs while working to convince the attackers to lift the siege. Masud did so; he returned to his former friends, provided them with bad advice and worked to sow discord. Before long, the siege was abandoned and Islam was saved.

It is very important for us to understand the doctrine and practice of taqiyya as it pertains to Islam's relationship to the Western world. Always keep these two things in mind: first, Islam actually codifies deceit. And more importantly, Islam demands deception in war and Islam is always at war against the non-Muslim world - until Islam is universally respected.

In yet another example, Mohammed was angered by the opposition of a certain Jew named Ka'b bin Al-Ashraf. This man had composed unflattering poems about Mohammed and his religion but had not raised a hand against the prophet or any other Muslim. According to the Hadith, Mohammed complained about the man's "abuse" saying, "Who is willing to kill Ka'b bin Al-Ashraf who has hurt Allah and His Apostle?" Thereupon Muhammad bin Maslama got up saying, "O Allah's Apostle! Would you like that I kill him?" The prophet said, "Yes," Muhammad bin Maslama said, "Then allow me to say a (false) thing (i.e. to deceive Kab). "The prophet said, "You may say it" (5.59. 369).

Maslama succeeded in getting close to Ka'b by leading him to believe he was in sympathy with his anti-Muslim views. Then, when the opportunity presented itself, Maslama and a companion killed

Ka'b, beheaded him and brought the gory trophy to the prophet of Allah. It is reported that upon seeing the head of Ka'b in the hand of Maslama, Mohammed cried out "Allah Akbar!" Sound familiar?

Thus, Mohammed is not only an advocate of deceit but the orchestrator of cold-blooded murder. Think about it; the Jew Ka'b never did anything against Mohammed and his new religion. Yes, he said things - but that does not justify physical violence against the man let alone murder. And lest we forget, this sort of behavior remains common today. Violent riots have ensued and people have lost their lives, gunned down simply for drawing cartoon pictures of Mohammed. Truly, to a devout Muslim, "oppression" of Islam through ridicule is worse than the murder of those who oppress by ridicule (cf. Koran, sura 2.190). Clearly, freedom of speech and expression of views contrary to Islam have no place whatsoever in the "religion of peace."

CONCLUSION, A STATE OF WAR

Islam is at war with the American way of life. Indeed, Islam is at war with every civilized society on the face of the earth. The war propagated by Islam throughout the world is a political war, a cultural war and a shooting war. All three aspects of this war are currently taking place in the United States of America.

A Political War

Our current federal government seems more than happy to accommodate the political ambitions of Islam. In addition to appointing Muslims to positions of power,[25] non-Muslim members of government do their level best to make the federal bureaucracy a Muslim friendly place. For instance, in the aftermath of the San Bernardino terrorist attack in which fourteen Americans were killed and twenty-one wounded, Loretta Lynch, United States Attorney General, forcefully warned that any and all anti-Muslim speech would be swiftly and severely prosecuted by the United States government.[26] This is in keeping with the words of our own president who said "the future must not belong to those who slander the prophet, of Islam."[27] But according to Islamic teaching, any disagreement or rejection of Islam is to disrespect Mohammed. In short, our own United States government is already pandering to the desires of the Islamists. We can expect this to continue unless we do something about it. It is time for Americans to demand true representative leadership.

A Cultural War

It was recently reported that the largest school district in Maryland removed all references to Christian and Jewish holidays on the school calendar. This was in response to the insistence of local Muslims to include Islamic holy days as well.[28] It may seem the Muslims lost this round since the school calendar still won't acknowledge Muslim holidays. But anytime Islam is successful in eroding traditional American values they've won that battle. This is just one example of the culture war Islam is waging against the American way of life. It is becoming commonplace to see news images of Muslim mobs here in America screaming out threats against any and all who would dare to observe a traditional custom that is offensive to the followers of Mohammed. Like every other leftist organization, Islamists maintain constant pressure on their opponents. Leftism is known for extreme discourtesy and it is no different for Muslims in America. Yes, the so-called moderate Muslims tut-tut the behavior of their more ideologically consistent Islamic brothers and sisters but nothing is actually done about it.

A Shooting War

Americans are finally waking up to the fact that Islamic jihadists as are among us and more than ready to pull the trigger on behalf of Allah and his apostle. Our civil leaders try to tell us that Islamic attacks are just workplace violence"[29] [30] and attempt to shift attention to the violent behavior of the most recent homegrown white male who has gone on a rampage. Yet, I think the terror attack in San Bernardino California has opened the eyes of a significant number of Americans. There is a growing call for "something to be done." Hopefully we will be able to find and elect leadership at the county, state and federal level that will take an aggressive stand against Islamic ideology. Until then, we must be prepared to fend for ourselves. Until then, we must do everything we can to survive the next terrorist attack or stop it before it begins.

[1]Statement by President Barack Hussein Obama, "Statement by the President on the Occasion of Eid-al-Fitr," July 27, 2014, retrieved on December 25, 2015: online at https://www.whitehouse.gov/the-press-office/2014/07/27/statement-president-occasion-eid-al-fitr

[2]"The word 'Hadith' comes from the Arabic word meaning news or information. It has a special meaning in Islam. It refers to the sayings and doings of prophet, Mohammed and the actions he approved." Ghulam Sarwar, *Islam Beliefs And Teachings*, (1980, London: The Muslim Educational Trust, 2003), 196.

[3]Ghulam Sarwar, *Islam Beliefs And Teachings*, 118.

[4]Ghulam Sarwar, *Islam Beliefs And Teachings*, (1980, London: The Muslim Educational Trust, 2003), 118.

[5]Ghulam Sarwar, *Islam Beliefs And Teachings*, 82.

[6]Suzanne Haneef, *What Everyone Should Know about Islam and Muslims*, (Chicago: Library of Islam, 1996), 27.

[7]

[8]Ghulam Sarwar, *Islam Beliefs And Teachings*, (1980, London: The Muslim Educational Trust, 2003), 31,

brackets added.

[9]Ali Dashti, *23 Years: A Study of the Prophetic Career of Mohammed*, (Costa Mesa: Mazda Publishers, 1994), 98.

[10]Ali Dashti, *23 Years*, 28, 48.

[11]Ghulam Sarwar, *Islam Beliefs*, 196.

[12]Sahih al-Bukhari. (n.d.). In Wikipedia. Retrieved December 6, 2015, from https://en.wikipedia.org/wiki/Sahih_al-Bukhari

[13]Ali Dashti, *23 Years: A Study of the Prophetic Career of Mohammed*, (Costa Mesa: Mazda Publishers, 1994), 53.

[14]Robert Spencer, *The Complete Infidel's Guide to the Koran*, (Washington DC: Regnery Publishing, Inc, 2009), 46.

[15]Spencer, *Infidel's Guide*, 55.

[16]Anthony Esolen, *The Politically Incorrect Guide to Western Civilization*, (Washington DC: Regnery Publishing Incorporated, 2008), 141.

[17]Robert Spencer, *The Complete Infidel's Guide to the Koran*, (Washington DC: Regnery Publishing, Inc, 2009), 186.

[18]Albert Hourani *A History of the Arab Peoples*, (Cambridge MA: Harvard University Press, 1991), 22-23.

[19] Lizzie Dearden, "Isis 'fatwa' on female sex slaves tells militants how and when they can rape captured women and girls," The Independent News, December 29, 2015: online at, http://www.independent.co.uk/news/world/middle-east/isis-fatwa-on-female-sex-slaves-tells-militants-how-and-when-they-can-rape-captured-women-and-girls-a6789036.html

[20] Erik Von Kuehnelt-Leddihin, *Leftism Revisited: From De Sade and Marx to Hitler and Pol Pol*, (Washington DC: Regnery Publications, 1991).

[21] Sayyid Qutb, *Milestones*, (New Delhi India: Islamic Book Service Ltd., 2002), 72.

[22] Sayyid Qutb, *Milestones*, 73.

[23] Hourani *A History of the Arab Peoples*, 47.

[24] Robert Spencer, *The Complete Infidel's Guide to the Koran*, (Washington DC: Regnery Publishing, Inc, 2009), 194.

[25] Leon Puissegur, "Sharia Advisors - Barack Obama's Muslim Appointees in High Security Positions," *Freedom Outpost*, April 29, 2014: online at http://freedomoutpost.com/2014/04/sharia-advisers-barack-obamas-muslim-appointees/#2whF2Aet09F Esfk3.99

[26] Bob Unruh, "AG Lynch vows to prosecute 'anti-Muslim' speech" *World Net Daily*, December 12, 2015: online at, http://www.wnd.com/2015/12/ag-lynch-vows-to-prosecute-anti-muslim-speech/#osUgU4ZmDoo4YP5X.99

[27] . From a speech delivered to the United Nations General Assembly, September 25, 2012: online at https://

www.white house.gov/the-press-office/2012/09/25/remarks-president-un-general-assembly

[28] Deborah Hastings, "Maryland's largest school district to drop all religious holidays from calendar," *The New York Daily News*, November 12, 2014: online at, http://www.nydailynews.com /news/national/md-school-district-bans-religious-holidays-calendars-article-1.2008745

[29] Cortney O'Brien, "Five Years After Callous 'Workplace Violence' Designation, Fort Hood Victims Awarded Purple Hearts" *TownHall.com*, April 10, 2015: online at, http://townhall.com/tipsheet/cortneyobrien/2015/04/10/fort-hood-purple-hearts-n1983459

[30] Gregory Korte, "Terrorism is 'possible' in San Bernardino shootings, Obama says" *USA Today*, December 3, 2015: online at, http://www.usatoday.com/story/news/politics/2015/12/03/obama-terrorism-possible-calif-shooting/76719644/

ABOUT THE AUTHOR

David Eric Williams

David 'Eric' Williams has ministered throughout the Mountain-West region of the United States since 1988. He holds a BA from the University of the State of New York (History/ Sociology) an MA from the Southern California Graduate School of Theology (Theology) and an MAR from Liberty University School of Divinity (Biblical Studies, Graduate With High Distinction). He is ordained with the Conservative Congregational Christian Conference. Eric and his wife have been part of the home-school counter culture for over 35 years.

BOOKS BY THIS AUTHOR

An Introduction To The Book Of Ruth

The book of Ruth tells the tale of women in crisis. The Primary characters in the story are widows - and one of them is a foreigner. In the world of ancient Israel, no one was more vulnerable than Ruth and Naomi. Nonetheless, the main characters are shown to be wise, resourceful and courageous. Against all odds, they realize the blessings of God and secure a special place in the history of God's people.

Baptism Basics: Essays Concerning The Nature, Meaning And Subjects Of Baptism

According to the Bible, the doctrine of baptism is elementary to the Christian faith. This means even immature Christians should understand it. However, different points of view about the sacrament of baptism have persisted in the church for hundreds of years. It is the hope of the author that the Holy Spirit will use this booklet to help you in your study of Scripture concerning the elementary principal of baptism.

Men Of Issachar: Understand The Times, Know What To Do

According to Webster's dictionary a crisis is a "decisive moment or an unstable or crucial time or state of affairs" in history. It is fashionable to suggest the early 21st century is a time of crisis. We are told by our leadership that crisis is at every hand. Indeed, when crisis does not materialize as quickly or as violently as one might expect it seems civil leadership is not adverse to creating "crisis."

However, we are in the midst of crisis. The situation we face today is not economic, environmental, political or sociological. Instead, it is a crisis of leadership at the most elementary level. It is a crisis requiring a dramatic cultural shift in order to correct the course of history. As things now stand we are headed for disaster. Indeed, we are experiencing the slow unfolding of disaster all around us even today.

Shine Forth As The Sun: The Messianic Reign In Parable According To Matthew's Gospel

The kingdom of God: when will it begin? What are its characteristics? Who will be a part of it? Drawing from the "kingdom is like" parables of our Lord Jesus Christ, Pastor D. Eric Williams examines these questions and more in this collection of sermons concerning the kingdom of God according to Matthew's Gospel

Real Faith: Studies In The Epistle Of James

The Epistle of James is all about Faith - real faith, living faith, active faith. Like the apostle Paul, James would have us work out our salvation with fear and trembling. This book endeavors to show just how that is done. According to James' epistle, real faith is based upon certain presuppositions. True faith finds joy in hardship. Faith brings unity in the body; it engenders self control; it benefits the individual and the world at large. 'Real Faith, Studies In The Epistle Of James' will enable you to read the letter of James with fresh eyes and allow you to apply this misunderstood book to your walk of faith.

The End Was Near: End Times Bible Prophecy Made Simple

Are we living in the Last Days? Are the End Times upon us? Many popular writers confidently say we are the terminal generation - but is that what the Bible says? Find out in this introductory study of biblical eschatology by Pastor and writer D. Eric Williams. In this brief overview of the topic, Pastor Williams reveals the proper approach to interpreting End Time passages and provides the tools necessary for understanding biblical eschatology. End Times truth begins with "The End Was Near" where you'll find End Times Bible prophecy made simple, without the End Times fiction!

Apocalypse: An Explanatory Rendering Of The Revelation That Will Forever Alter Your Understanding Of The Tribulation, The Beast And The End Times

The Revelation has long been a source of mystery to Christian and non Christian alike. Thought by many to be a prophecy concerning the end of the world, The Revelation stirs the emotions of all who read it. But has this cryptic book been properly understood? Is it a prophecy of doom or is it a prophecy of hope - or both? Now for the first time in modern history, the message of The Revelation has been made clear. Agree or disagree with the interpretation of Pastor and writer D. Eric Williams, but be sure that upon reading this explanatory rendering of The Revelation, your understanding of the Tribulation, the Beast and the End Times will forever be changed.

A Catechism Of The Thirty-Nine Articles Of Religion: Or The Confession Of Faith Put Forth By The Church Of England With Scripture Proofs

A Catechism Of The Thirty-Nine Articles Of Religion, Or The Confession Of Faith Put Forth By The Church Of England, With Scripture Proofs For The Use Of Schools And Junior Students, By J. W., Second Edition corrected and enlarged Griffith & Farran, Warren & Son, 1877.

Printed in Great Britain
by Amazon